Surviving Suicide Loss

You Are Not Alone

By: Randall Stepp

This book is dedicated to the memory of my son and best friend.

Brandon Tyler Stepp

Contents

Surviving Suicide Loss

Silent Killer

Suicide so elusive.
Lies hidden in plain sight.
Can stalk its prey for decades.
Or devour you in a night.

It begins as a whisper.
Grows louder day by day.
It sells itself as an option.
While omitting the price you pay.

Meditations on the consequences.
Are distracted by its screams.
Feeding off human misery.
Thriving on broken dreams.

It seduces you with the drama.
Picturing reactions in your mind.
Numbs you to the impact.
On those you leave behind.

Deadly thoughts and circumstance.
Combine with deadly force.
A future of hope and happiness.
Has taken a different course.

A precious life has ended.
Through deception and deceit.
Another family has fallen victim.
Suicides mission is complete

About the Author

 My name is Randall Stepp and I am a survivor of suicide. Prior to losing my fifteen year old son Brandon, I harbored no aspirations of becoming an author. I was contently living out my life until suicide walked in and changed everything. In the wake of Brandon's suicide, I began to write poetry. This collection of poetry later grew into a book entitled "Losing a Son to Suicide, A poetic journey through grief". Now with this book, I intend to share what I have learned since losing my son. I am not claiming to be an expert on any subject. I am merely someone that has faced what you are facing. I have known the unique pain and anguish that come with losing a loved one to suicide. My journey began on October 14, 2010. That is the day my old life ended and I became a survivor of suicide, it is also the day that I began my journey through suicide grief. My only credentials for writing this book were earned in the months and years since that day. I don't have any clever advice to make the terrible pain go away, or some magic phrase that will answer all of your questions. All I have to offer you is reassurance that what you're feeling is completely normal for someone grieving a loss to suicide. I will also try to inspire you, to take this tragic loss and use it as a catalyst to live a life that is a tribute to your loved ones memory. Lastly, I intend to keep reminding you that you are not alone in your suffering. I am walking the same path as you, I am merely a few years ahead of you on my journey. I hope that one day in the future, you will be strong enough to offer your hand to a fellow survivor that is just entering into this secret world of hurt, known as suicide loss.

Introduction

t is all just a bad dream, it is just too terrible to be real. I remember repeating those phrases in the first days and weeks after the suicide of my fifteen year old son Brandon. My life wasn't supposed to end up like this. I had plans for the future and now suicide had entered my life and rearranged everything. Brandon was my only child so losing him meant the loss of countless expectations. He would never go to college or get married, and grandchildren were something that would never be a part of my life. Simply losing a child would have been difficult enough, but once you add suicide to the equation it can almost seem insurmountable. However, it is possible to weather this storm and learn to live again. On the proceeding pages I will attempt to both console and encourage you. I will share with you what I have learned since becoming a suicide survivor in October of 2010. It is a long difficult road and not a journey that I would wish upon anyone, but others have made it and so will you. Just keep breathing in and breathing out. Try to simply live from moment to moment, because anything more will only serve to discourage you in the beginning. However, if you face this grief and don't try to avoid it, you will start to lay the foundations for a life after suicide. A new normal, which sadly will no longer include your loved one, but with their memory serving as your guide. You will make it, and you will discover that you are much stronger than you had ever imagined. It is my hope that by reading this book, you will learn that you are not alone on this painful and harrowing journey.

That Terrible Day

O ctober 14, before 2010 that date was just another day on the calendar, but all that changed when suicide turned that day into a date that now divides my life. That is the day my old normal ended and I began my painful journey to forge a new normal.

It was just an ordinary Thursday in October. Outside it was sunny and bright, but little did I know of the storm that was approaching. I went to work as usual and had a normal routine day, but for my son it was anything but a pleasant day. His name was Brandon Tyler Stepp and he was my son and best friend. He had a smile that could light up any room and the most beautiful blue eyes you had ever seen. He was fifteen and had recently broken up with his first serious girlfriend. I didn't find out until after the fact, but he had been texting her and threatening to harm himself. I will never know exactly what he was thinking, but I believe he never intended to follow through on his threats, until his back was placed against the wall. This is my recollection of what happened on that terrible day. When he arrived home from wrestling practice, I could instantly sense that something was wrong. He looked worried and scared, a look that is forever burned into my memory. I asked him several times what was wrong, but he just said he didn't feel well and went upstairs. His bedroom and guitar room were upstairs so this was nothing out of the ordinary. It was during this time that he must have gotten my rifle out of the closet and taken it to his guitar room. While he was upstairs, I was discussing with my wife which restaurant we should go to. Once we decided, we called for Brandon and he came downstairs to go with us. As we were nearing the front door, the doorbell rang. Brandon just casually turned and ran upstairs, and for some reason I ran after him. I guess I could just sense that something was terribly wrong. As I was nearing the top of the stairs, I heard the sound of a gunshot. As I opened the door, I watched helplessly as my son fell to the floor. From that point on, it all seems like an out of body experience. I could hear myself screaming and pleading with Brandon to stay awake. Me and my wife performed CPR until the ambulance arrived. He was taken to our local hospital and then airlifted to University hospital in Louisville, KY. In a few hours we had lost Brandon forever. Only after the fact, did the events of that day start to make sense. We later learned that on the way home from wrestling practice, Brandon had received a text from his ex-girlfriend. She told him that she and her mother were coming to our house to tell us of his threats. We don't know what prompted her to do this on that day, because his texts were not recent. We speculate that she discovered he had a new girlfriend and acted out of jealousy. However we will never know for sure, and now it really doesn't matter. Brandon is gone and no amount of animosity is going to change that. To understand why Brandon reacted like he did, you need to know a few things about him. He was a classic overachiever. He excelled in almost everything he did. He maintained a 4.0 GPA while taking honors classes. In short, he held himself to a much higher standard. He expected more from himself than he did anyone else. He must have felt like his whole world of perfection was crashing down on him. That is why he looked so worried and scared when he arrived home that day. I'm sure he thought that we would be disappointed in him, that we would think less of him somehow. Nothing could have been further from the truth. As I will describe later in the book, I truly would have understood.

I still remember that lonely drive home from the hospital. It felt so surreal to be coming home and to not have my child with me. I felt as if I had failed as a parent. When my son needed me the most, I was not there. I will never know why he didn't confide in me that day. We always talked about everything, but I guess he just felt too embarrassed to share his struggle with me. Now that is simply another question to be added to the multitude of others that I struggle with, another question that I will carry with me, until one day I see Brandon again. When that day finally comes, I will no longer need those answers, because then I will have my precious son back in my arms. Well, that is my story and like you I have told it countless times. In the beginning, you too will have that strong urge to share your story. You will need to keep telling it over and over until you no longer feel compelled to do so. I think that this is simply our minds way of finding an explanation for what happened. Once you are able to piece together a story that you can live with, this urge to share your story will begin to subside. There's no timetable as to when that will be. Take as long as you need and don't get discouraged if you have setbacks. Just keep in mind that this is all perfectly normal for someone grieving a loss to suicide.

Brandon and I shortly before his suicide.

The Club

You are now the member of an unfortunate group, an unlucky club of people that have suffered a loss to suicide. It is a club that none of us requested to join, and all of its members would gladly relinquish their memberships if only we could. Unfortunately that is not an option. We must face what has happened and somehow get through it. It is an arduous journey that all suicide survivors must endure, and don't think that it can be avoided. You cannot go around it or over it, it must be gone through and experienced in order to provide you with the closure that you need in order to carry on. Note that I said carry on, not move on. You can never just move on after the loss of a loved one. You must incorporate your loss into who you are, and carry on with the business of life. A business that continues on around you, regardless of what's going on in your personal world. I still vividly remember that first morning after losing Brandon. The birds were singing, and the school bus was running as usual. I felt like stepping outside and screaming at the top of my lungs. How dare the world just keep on turning when my son was gone. Didn't they know what a treasure the world had lost. That realization that life goes on, is one of the cruelest parts of losing someone you love. To the world they were just one person, but to you they were the whole world. Like all the other facets of grief, this resentment of life continuing on will eventually subside. Although you will still have occasional flare ups, perhaps whenever you see something new that your loved one will never get to experience. I know that I feel that way whenever I hear a new song on the radio. Brandon really loved music and it hurts to hear something that he would have liked. Rational or not, you will experience similar feelings at some point. Just don't get discouraged, you are grieving and you will be dealing with grief to some degree for the rest of your life.

Grief Squared

Where did everyone go? You might find yourself asking that question in the months after suffering a loss to suicide. In the immediate aftermath of your loved ones suicide, your house was always filled with people offering their support. Now several months later, the visits and the support have suddenly disappeared. It is as if everyone simultaneously agreed that your grieving should now be over, that you should simply get over it and go back to your old life. What they fail to realize, is the fact that your old life is no longer there for you to return to. Suicide has entered your life and forever altered who you are, and it will take some time for you to get back on your feet again. You cannot simply rush through the stages of grief, and emerge a few months later completely healed and back to yourself once again. Our society as a whole has very unrealistic expectations when it comes to grief, and these expectations are even more unrealistic when it comes to suicide loss. Grief is an arduous journey that can take you years to complete, and when you add the complications of suicide to the equation it can take even longer. As suicide survivors we have to navigate through a maze of questions to even begin the grieving process, and by the time we finally come to terms with our loved one's suicide, the well of support has dried up. People don't understand that suicide grief is the emotional equivalent of having your leg amputated, and then being told to keep on walking as usual. With the support of a prosthetic you may eventually walk again, but never in the same way you once did.

In the days and months to follow, you will discover that grief does not present itself in a neat orderly manner. You don't simply complete one phase and then graduate on to the next. Instead it is more of a repeating cycle that with each passing will become more and more bearable. These cycles can take months or years to complete. It all depends on who you lost and your relationship with that person, but please don't let that discourage you. I still grieve the loss of my son and at the same time I'm able to carry on with the day to day business of life. Just because you're grieving that doesn't mean you're not living. As a parent that has lost a child, I believe that I will never fully recover from my son's death, although it is a very different grief from what I faced in those first days and months after losing Brandon. I am now able to laugh again without feeling guilty for it, and with time you will get to the same place. Just be patient with yourself and celebrate those little victories you have each day. Which in the beginning of your grief, can be as simple as getting out of bed.

Suicide grief brings with it a myriad of emotions. I think it should be referred to as grief squared, because almost every aspect of grief is amplified. One of the most exaggerated emotions is anger. You may be angry with your loved one for leaving you, or even angry at God for letting this happen. It is just important that you know this anger will come at some point. Most of my anger was indirect, meaning it was not directed at Brandon. Which is normally the case with bereaved parents. If your loss is a sibling or spouse you will probably direct your anger at your loved one. There is no need to feel guilty or ashamed when this happens. It is an important part of grieving a loss to suicide. I remember getting very angry at other drivers during those first months, and wait until you hear someone remark that they are having a bad day. You want to sit them down and explain to them what a bad day really looks like. One thing that still gets me angry to this day is observing a parent completely ignoring their child. I wish that they could understand what a precious gift our children actually are, but they haven't had their eyes opened by tragedy as we have. They can't imagine what it would be like to desperately want to hug your child and not be able to, or to lie in bed at night worrying that you will forget the sound of your child's voice. They are like we once were, oblivious to just how quickly it can all be lost. So just realize that there will always be things that will draw your ire as a suicide survivor, and when this anger comes, you need to express it. Buy some old dishes and smash them in the backyard, or simply go outside and scream at the top of your lungs. Just let it out, if it is suppressed it will surface at some point. It is much healthier to have small controlled releases of this anger than it is to have complete meltdowns, because those huge outbursts of anger can be very damaging to your personal relationships. Since this anger usually ends up being directed at those you love the most, and right now you don't need any additional losses in your life, so try to find some non-destructive outlets for your anger. Eventually this anger will start to subside and you will begin to feel more like yourself again. Until then, just be patient and realize that this anger is simply another obstacle that you must face on your journey through grief.

Guilt is another emotion that you will surely face as a suicide survivor. In those first few months, it can be almost overwhelming. You will feel guilty for things both said and unsaid. You will keep replaying the events surrounding your loved one's suicide, searching for anything that you may have missed. In short, you will examine every interaction between you and your loved one, simply looking for things to feel guilty about. And your guilt will not be confined to just the suicide itself. It will also have a huge impact on your entire grieving process. I remember even feeling guilty for eating, during those first few months of grief, and prepare to be knocked down by guilt the first time you smile or laugh again. Just understand that all of this guilt you're feeling is perfectly normal and healthy. You will always be harder on yourself than you are anyone else. You have lost someone very dear and you are now looking for someone to blame. That is when guilt steps in and points its finger in your direction, but don't lose heart. Over time these feelings of guilt will start to subside. It will not happen overnight though, it is a very gradual process. Until then, just try to go easy on yourself. You know that you would have done anything to prevent your loved ones suicide, and as long as you keep telling yourself that. It will help to keep those guilty feelings at bay.

There are things that you need to remember when grieving and there are things that you need to forget. Should is a word that you need to eliminate from your vocabulary during the earlier stages of grief. Every friend and family member will tell you exactly what you should or shouldn't be doing, and sometimes even complete strangers will offer up their opinions on how you should be grieving. Just do what you can, when you can. If you feel like cleaning the house, do it. If you are just simply too drained from the ravages of grief, then come back to it whenever you are able to, just giving yourself permission to say no, can help to eliminate stress during an already too stressful time. Just remember these important words. "Don't should on yourself, and don't let anyone else should on you either." That's a phrase I've heard countless times at the survivors of suicide meetings that I attend. I have found it to be very simple, but sage advice.

Grieving any death is difficult, but a loss to suicide is even more complicated. In addition to missing your loved one, you are left with so many questions and the sad realization that most of your questions will never receive an answer. I still remember those first few weeks. I was constantly replaying the events surrounding Brandon's suicide. I think some part of me believed that if I could solve this riddle, then Brandon would return to me. It was during this time that I discovered writing poetry. Just the act of putting my thoughts down on paper seem to help ease the sometimes overwhelming pressure I felt. If you haven't already attempted it, I would highly recommend that you try some form of writing. It can be something as simple as a list of things that you wish you would have done differently, or you could write your loved one a letter simply expressing how you feel. No one has to ever read what you write, this is strictly for your eyes only. You will probably find that it will help to temporarily calm the storm of emotions that you are experiencing, because during the earlier stages of grief, even a few minutes of distraction can be a lifesaver. I remember referring to myself as a homesick child early in my grief. As long as my mind was occupied, I was fine. It was during those quiet times that the grief seemed almost unbearable.

Nighttime is when grief will hit you the hardest. It is during this time that all of your guilt and regrets will come to visit. You will dissect every single memory that you have of your loved one, looking for that one hidden clue that you missed. You know the one, the one that could have prevented your loss to suicide. When these thoughts hit me,

I find solace in knowing that if given a chance. I would have walked through hell and back to prevent this nightmare from occurring. But no matter what you do, this second guessing is just another inevitable part of grieving a loss to suicide. It is during this time that sleep becomes a precious commodity. Sleep is your only escape from all of the pain and anguish that you are feeling, but this escape comes at a price, and the price of sleep is reawakening. Waking up to the sad reality that you have lost your loved one, and that realization is the first thought that crosses your mind every time you wake up. It is almost like losing your loved one all over again. I know for the first year or so, that was always the first thing on my mind. Now, it is more of a constant realization. A cold hard fact that you are aware of, but doesn't quite carry the same sharp piercing pain that it once did. So if you are just beginning your long journey through grief. Rest assured that at some point, nighttime will again become bearable. When that is will vary greatly for all of us, but just know that it will happen. Until then just try to focus on all those happy memories that your loved one brought into your life, and speaking of those happy memories. If you suffer from flashbacks, as I once did. Try picking out one special memory and think of it every time you're confronted with a flashback.

Eventually you will train your mind to focus on that happy memory and lessen the impact of those horrific images. I know in my case it took me over a year to ease the intensity of the images that I was struggling with, so just be patient and realize that this exercise will take some time. However at some point, you will be able to close your eyes and not be faced with those startling images.

Another thing that I remember about the earlier stages of grief was the feeling that I was going insane. I remember walking into a room to retrieve something and just standing there completely dumbfounded as to what it was. I would set my drink down and forget where I put it. I remember one incident that occurred shortly after I returned to work. I parked my car and forgot to set the parking brake. I came out to find my car sitting in a parking lot on the other side of the street, so please be careful during those early months of grief. Your mind is still in shock which will wreak absolute havoc on your memory. And your memory loss is not the only thing that will make you feel insane. You might notice the familiar scent of your loved one and feel like their near, or you may believe that you have seen them in a shopping center. I remember when I would constantly look at license plates and add the numbers. I don't know exactly what I was looking for, but I did it for months. So if you find yourself doing something that doesn't quite make sense. I wouldn't worry about it, unless it is adversely affecting your day to day life. And if that is the case, it would be wise to see a professional and get their opinion.

What's next? How do I build a life again without my loved one? These are inevitable questions that you will ask yourself after suffering a loss to suicide. You feel as if you are the only one in the world to ever face such an obstacle. But I'm here to let you know that others have made it through this ordeal, and that you are not alone on your journey. I remember during those first few weeks, and at one point I went and looked at myself in the mirror. I expected some sort of monster to be staring back at me, but it was just me, looking like I always looked. At the time I resented the fact that I could lose my entire world and still look the same, but that is one thing about grief. It is not logical, it is purely emotional. You just have to embrace whatever your feeling at the time and not fight it. Eventually logic will return and you will become more like the person you once were. You will never be the same, but you will emerge from this, and when you do. You will be a kinder and gentler version of the person you were before. Someone that is a lot more empathetic to the suffering of others and quicker to offer a hand to eliminate it. When all is said and done, you will construct a new normal in place of the old and you will learn to smile and laugh again. This new normal will never compare to the old, but life will regain some semblance of normality. The time between now and then is when you will earn the title of suicide survivor. So until then, just keep living one moment at a time. Keep putting one foot in front of the other, and eventually, you will be strong enough to offer your hand to another survivor that is just beginning their journey. It will not happen overnight, but it will happen. Until then, you just need to keep reminding yourself that you are not alone.

The Stigma Descends

Almost immediately after losing a loved one to suicide. You will feel the stigma of suicide begin to descend upon you and affect almost every part of your life. You will be tempted to avoid certain places and people. You will feel embarrassment and shame when telling people what caused the death of your loved one. Suicide carries with it the historical baggage and religious implications that set it apart from all other causes of death. Survivors of suicide have historically been treated terribly by society due to ignorance and fear, and the religious implications bring into question whether your loved one resides in Heaven or hell. All of these factors contribute to the undeniable shame that survivors of suicide are faced with, and the only weapon that we have in this war against the stigma of suicide is speaking out. Don't hide the fact that your loved one died by suicide. By sharing, you will make it easier for the next person to speak out and break their silence. For far too long we have let the guilt and shame of suicide cast its ugly shadow on the memories of our loved ones. Only by speaking out, can we drag suicide out of the darkness and into the daylight.

Our loved ones simply made an irreversible mistake. The circumstances and factors surrounding that mistake are different for everyone, but we should not let one mistake define our loved ones entire life. This was just one brief and fleeting moment in their life, and if given a second chance and a clear mind. They would likely not suffer the same fate, so whenever possible. I am open about what happened to Brandon, and more often than not. Others will share with me how they too have lost someone to suicide, and if enough of us share our stories. One day we will be able to finally defeat the ugly stigma of suicide.

When you are telling others of your loved one and how they died, do you feel the need to explain how they were still a good person despite their suicide? I know that I used to do that almost every time I would speak about losing Brandon. I felt as if it were my responsibility as a father, to help defend my son's memory. When people hear that someone has died by suicide, they will form a mental image of what they think that person was like, and that image rarely bears any resemblance to that of our loved one. I know that in the past, I was guilty of the same thing. I would always picture a miserable soul that had never known true happiness, and I knew firsthand that this was not the case because of my own experience. I think that is one reason the stigma of suicide hits us so hard. We know what other people are thinking, because at one time we used to think exactly the same thing, and although it is very difficult. You need to realize that it really doesn't matter what other people think of our loved ones. Their opinions will never be able to change who our loved ones really were. Even though it is hard to accept, there are some people that will always imagine our loved one's as faceless victims that possessed some sort of defect, which caused them to complete suicide. By doing so, they can deceive themselves into thinking that suicide could never impact their life. It is this fear that continues to feed the stigma of suicide. This fear can also cause certain friends and family members to suddenly start avoiding you. They will act as if you have contracted some strange virus, which could cause suicide to spread to their families. It might not be rational, but believe me you will encounter this with some people. Try not to take it personally if you experience this, it is simply another one, of the many evils created by the stigma of suicide.

It was also the stigma surrounding suicide that I blame for one of my biggest failings as a father. At the age of 18, I attempted suicide after a fight with my then girlfriend and now wife Sherri. If only I could have shed the stigma of suicide sooner. Then it is very possible that I could have opened the door for my son to confide in me. Well, it is now too late for my story to help my son, but maybe it can help to offer you some important insights into the mindset of someone that attempts suicide. I was eighteen years old and Sherri was my first serious girlfriend. We had been fighting one night and for some reason, I remarked that I was going to kill myself. She immediately changed her demeanor, anger quickly turned to concern. Well this reaction only served to encourage me to keep using the threat for shock value. I believe a lot of young people are like I was. They are seduced by all of the drama surrounding suicide. I remember imagining Sherri's reaction and picturing how sorry she would be after I was gone. I never took the time to fully comprehend the finality of the act that I was considering. I was not an unhappy person, I wasn't in terrible emotional pain. I was simply behaving like an immature young man that was seeking attention. I don't remember even once stopping to consider the impact my actions would have on all those left behind. My parents would have been left to try and reconcile my suicide with the son that they knew. Well my threats continued until they started to lose their shock value, and I was no longer receiving the reaction that I was seeking. In response, I chose to up the ante in the very dangerous game that I was playing with suicide. To do this, I snuck a bottle of sleeping pills out of my mother's medicine cabinet. Now with the means to follow through, I knew that I would be taken seriously again. My attempt occurred one evening following a particularly bad day at my first job. Sherri and I were arguing later that evening and in a moment of anger, I grabbed the pills and quickly swallowed the entire bottle. I immediately came to my senses after taking the pills. It was as if someone turned on a light switch and I finally realized the permanency of my actions. I remember telling Sherri to get me to the hospital, and by the time we arrived I was unconscious. Luckily they were able to pump my stomach and save my life. After that attempt, I have never even once considered suicide again. Sadly, my son did not get this second chance at life as I did. He was like most other young men that attempt suicide. He chose a much more lethal method and when such methods are used. All chances of having a change of heart are eliminated. Knowing all this, makes dealing with Brandon's suicide seem even more difficult. Not to mention the regret I feel, and while I still blame myself for not sharing my story. I now have a much better understanding of why I chose not to. The stigma of suicide is so strong that entire families will keep secrets as to the cause of a loved one's death. I now use my suicide attempt as a valuable source of inspiration for my poetry. Because of my experiences I am able to describe suicide from the inside out, as I do in my poem *Silent Killer*. Which is featured in the beginning of this book, so if you have let the stigma of suicide silence you. Please learn from my example and speak freely about suicide. It is only by stepping out of our comfort zones that we will ever defeat this insidious foe, and one day the stigma of suicide will finally be nothing more than an embarrassing footnote in history. It is a lofty goal and probably one that will not be realized in our lifetime, but we must strive for it anyway. It is my hope, that one day survivors of suicide will feel free to speak of their loved one's life and death without shame. When that dream finally becomes a reality, it will go a long way towards simplifying the all too complicated grief of suicide.

Rewriting History

After losing Brandon to suicide, I began attending a survivor's support group almost immediately. I lost Brandon on Thursday and was at the support group on the following Thursday. Now years later, I have probably attended over one hundred meetings. During that time, I have listened to the stories of countless survivors and one phenomenon that seems to occur quite frequently. Is that people will gradually convince themselves that their loved ones were destined to die by suicide. That their whole life was merely an act, a charade meant to fool others into believing that they were happy. This tendency always bothers me, as someone that has survived a suicide attempt. I realize how very close I was to having other people decide whether my happiness was authentic or not. Was I merely smiling to hide the deep hurt and pain that were going on inside me? I know that it is very tempting to just explain away the suicide by reimagining all of the memories of your loved one. Believe me, I understand the urge. Suicide does not make sense, and our analytical minds want answers, but at some point. We just have to accept that most of our questions will never get the satisfaction of an answer, and losing every happy memory of your loved one is much too high of a price to pay. In my case, I was merely an immature young man that was drawn in and held captive by the drama surrounding suicide. During this time, I still laughed and smiled. I felt real happiness and even made plans for the future, all while flirting with the idea of suicide. My childhood was full of happy memories that could have been forever tainted by the stain of suicide, so when it comes to Brandon's suicide. I try to isolate it from the rest of his life. It was simply an irreversible mistake that was made with no time to reflect on the consequences. As a result, I consider all of my happy memories with Brandon to be strictly off limits. Those are his memories, and I have no right to superimpose his suicide over top of them. When we do that we end up not only losing our loved one, but now we have also lost their precious memory as well. Suicide loss is difficult enough by itself. There is no need to add to this loss by rewriting your loved ones entire life story, in order to fit their final act. Our loved ones were so much more than just suicide victims. They were loving and caring individuals, and as such they deserve to have their memories preserved.

Signs

Before losing Brandon I never really gave much thought to life after death. I have always believed that there is a place called Heaven, but it wasn't something that I spent a lot of time thinking about. It is only after you lose someone very special to you, that it all begins to take on a much greater significance. I believe with suicide being such a traumatic and unexpected form of death. You really need some kind of reassurance that your loved one is still with you in some way. You just want some kind of sign to let you know that your loved one is in Heaven. I know this was definitely the case for me. I had heard too many people make cruel and ignorant comments about suicide victims. I had been told that it was the unforgivable sin and that all suicide victims would go to Hell. So when I lost Brandon, I couldn't help but to be worried about where he was spending eternity. This concern sent me on a quest to discover what the bible actually said about those who die by suicide, and to my surprise it really says nothing to condemn suicide. It does mention people dying by suicide, but it does so in a non-judgmental fashion. This is not to say that suicide is a good thing. We as survivors know all too well that is not the case. Suicide takes a precious life and leaves loved ones in absolute turmoil, but as far as the bible is concerned, it is just another form of death. Now, after a few years and a lot of soul searching, I believe that all we need to know about God can be summed up in three words. God is love, and those three words should help to remove all doubt and fear from your mind. If we as humans can forgive our loved ones for the pain that they have caused us. Then why would we worry about a God of love not doing the same thing. God knows that we are imperfect creatures that will make mistakes, so please remove this from your list of worries. Our loved ones are safe and at peace, and one day we will be reunited with them. Until that day, just keep this in mind. God is love, and love does not judge. With that being said, I will now get back to the subject of signs. Signs are simply God's way of giving us a perfectly timed hug. They can be as simple as seeing a rainbow when you're having a rough day or a song coming on the radio at just the right time. Signs help to reassure us that some part of our loved one lives on. I will never forget the first sign that I received from Brandon. It occurred about a week after I lost him. I was looking at his Facebook page and reading his profile, basically I was looking for clues. In his profile, he said that the bible was his favorite book and that Psalm 62 was his favorite verse. After reading that, I just went on with my day and never gave it a second thought, until a few days later when my wife and I were getting groceries. Since we didn't want to run into anyone we knew, we went to a nearby town. As we were driving back home, I noticed a church sign with Psalm 62 posted on it. My first sign from Brandon, turned out to be an actual sign. I took a picture of that sign and it can be found at the end of this chapter. Since then, I have had numerous signs from Brandon. I've had several comforting dreams and I regularly find feathers in the oddest places. The alarm clock in Brandon's room has sounded several times, even though it wasn't set, so if you're looking for a sign and haven't received one yet. Just be patient and it will happen. I believe that you just have to stop looking for it, and let it come to you. Just don't lose faith, in the coming months and years you will receive countless signs. You just have to be open to the idea of receiving them, and then they will come to you. I don't understand how or why that is, but after talking to numerous suicide survivors it seems to hold true.

My sign from Brandon.

Prelude to Poetry

O ut of every tragedy, there will arise a gift, it could be a previously unknown talent or a newfound purpose in life. Poetry is the gift that I discovered after Brandon's suicide. Prior to his death, I had never written poetry. Now, it has become a part of who I am, a coping mechanism that allows me to control those recurring thoughts that accompany a loss to suicide. This proved to be a lifesaver during those first few months after losing Brandon. It consumed both time and attention which allowed me to withstand the terrible onslaught of grief. Now years later, I have written countless poems that approach suicide and grief from almost every angle imaginable. Poetry allows me to express thoughts and emotions that otherwise would have no outlet. I can't imagine dealing with all of the baggage of suicide loss without it. On the following pages you will find my newest collection of poetry along with my reflections on each poem. In sharing my poetry, I hope to reassure you that the grief you are experiencing is completely normal. As suicide survivors we all struggle with the same thoughts and emotions, we all desperately want answers that we know we will never receive. I can't provide you with answers, but I can offer you the peace of mind that comes from knowing, you are not alone.

The first poem that I would like to share is *Survivor*. It is my attempt to convey the strong sense of community that exists between fellow survivors of suicide. They become less like friends and more like an extended family. Two survivors that are complete strangers can almost immediately bond with each other because of their shared suffering. That is the main reason that I still attend my local support group. Now it is more for the friendships than it is for the support. These people have seen me at the most desperate point in my life and were there to offer me a hand. I will always be grateful for the kindness and compassion they have shown me. If you have a support group available in your area, I would highly recommend that you attend. I still remember that feeling of relief after attending my first meeting. I could see firsthand that it was possible to survive the horror of suicide loss. Just witnessing someone that was a few years removed from their loss, was enough inspiration to get me through the next few weeks.

Survivor

I will come stand beside you.
And offer you my hand.
I have been where you are.
So I am able to understand.

I have experienced the same emotions.
The shock and the disbelief.
Felt the weight of the stigma.
That amplifies our grief.

I've been wide awake at midnight.
With worry weighing on my mind.
I've searched and searched for answers.
That I have discovered I'll never find.

But I have faith that you'll make it.
And find a reason to live once more.
You're now a suicide survivor.
You're not the person you were before.

Stolen is a poem that I believe accurately describes some of the elements of my son's suicide, especially the second stanza. I also believe it describes a lot of the aspects of almost every suicide, especially the line about concealing the implications. If only our loved ones could have seen beyond their own circumstances, and considered the pain and anguish that they were inflicting on us. However from my own experience, I know that this was something that never entered into the equation. They were focused so completely on what they were going through, that they never once stopped to consider the finality of their actions. I'm sure that if they had a second chance, they would all tell us the same thing. So please try to understand that their suicide was not about you, it was all about them and the circumstances that they were going through. It doesn't make you miss them any less, but I believe it does help to recognize that point.

Stolen

Like a thief in the night.
It robs you of your dreams.
Rearranges your reality.
Nothing's as it seems.

A permanent decision.
Without time to decide.
Rushed into self-destruction.
At the hands of suicide.

Conceals the implications.
That can never be undone.
Destroys another family.
Claims a daughter or a son.

The life that you once knew.
Has vanished without a trace.
It takes away your children.
Leaving questions in their place.

Mask is a poem that describes the way I felt for the first few years. On the outside everything looked like I was back to the person I once was, but inside I was barely holding it together. I remember feeling like I was going to explode if I didn't get that mask off and let my emotions out. Now I try not to hide behind my mask. If I'm feeling down, I try to be honest with myself and not disguise it. You can only hide your emotions for so long. Eventually they will surface and have to be dealt with. It is just much easier to do this sooner than later. Because early on, you will have a lot more people to support you. Time has a way of dispersing the crowd when it comes to suicide loss, so I encourage you to make every effort to be open with your grief. View it as an expression of love for the one you have lost. It is because you have loved so deeply, that you are now grieving so deeply.

Mask

Smile for the camera.
Don't show the way you feel.
Your grieving should be over.
Never mind you're hurting still.

Put on that happy face.
You've learned to wear so well.
Looking so normal on the outside.
As inside you go through hell.

Slip on that tattered mask.
You've worn for all these years.
Helps keep everyone feeling comfortable.
As it hides your hurt and tears.

Wondering how much longer.
You can endure this cruel charade.
Veiling your wounded soul behind the curtain.
As you live out your masquerade.

Reason is a poem that expresses my deeply held desire to help others in Brandon's memory. I hope that you too can use it as a source of inspiration, once you have started to heal. Just think of what a better world this would be, if we all viewed our lives as a living tribute to our loved ones. Now, my mission in life is to reassure as many suicide survivors as I can. To let them know that they are not alone in their struggles, that others have been down this lonely road and have lived to tell the tale. If I could only help to comfort just one fellow survivor, then I would consider my mission a success. I can still clearly remember that terrible feeling of isolation after Brandon's suicide, it is that memory which now serves to motivate me to help others. I can just picture that glorious day when I am finally reunited with Brandon in Heaven. I want to be able to look him in the eye and tell him that I became a better person because of the love I had for him, because of him I was able to see beyond myself and reach out to others. There are plenty of days when the thought of seeing Brandon again is all that keeps me going. Thankfully, I know in my heart that one day God will reunite us and all of those years spent without him, will be but a memory.

Reason

You're the reason I go on.
When I'm ready to give in.
I can hear your gentle voice.
Urging me to try again.

At times when all I can do.
Is mourn the fact you're gone.
I remember you're beside me.
Giving me the strength to carry on.

When life just seems so empty.
And I am struggling to get by.
I know I must honor your memory.
And promise I'll never let it die.

You'll live vicariously through me.
To make the world a better place.
And whenever I question the reason.
I'll close my eyes and see your face.

Affirmation is a poem that I wrote to motivate me during the holiday season. It was my attempt to snap myself out of a period of self-pity. I like to read it aloud whenever I'm feeling down and defeated. I can repeat those words and I get the sense that I will make it through this terrible trial. I hope that you will find it inspiring as well. I would encourage you to try and read this poem whenever you are struggling and feel like you are on the verge of giving up. Believe me, I know the feeling. Surviving suicide loss is the toughest thing that you will ever do in your life, but with time and effort you will emerge from this tragedy a much stronger person. You may still stumble and fall at times, but others have made it through this trial, and so will you.

Affirmation

Just take another breath.
Don't focus on the pain.
I will make it through this nightmare.
I will suffer through this strain.

I am going to survive this.
I will help others when I do.
It will be done in your honor.
Out of the love I have for you.

I must discover a new purpose.
Chart out a different course.
And find some positive outlet.
For all this sadness and remorse.

This tragedy will not define me.
I won't remain in this dark cloud.
I will emerge a better person.
Knowing my child would be so proud.

Talk of Tomorrow is a poem that was written specifically for bereaved parents. As parents, we constantly share the stories and accomplishments of our children. Until you lose your child, then it is like a party that you are no longer invited to. Even if you still speak of your child freely. You will find that others are hesitant to do so, which I believe is both due to the stigma of suicide and them not wanting to remind us of our loss. What they don't realize is that our deceased child is always on our mind, and hearing their name spoken is very important to us. We so desperately want to be reassured that our precious children will never be forgotten. That they will be remembered for the people they were, and not just for the manner in which they died. Suicide has already claimed their lives, we don't want it to do the same to their memories.

Talk of Tomorrow

You hear others talking about their children.
Discussing what is and what will be.
While you remain quiet and say nothing.
Because all those things you will never see.

You've lost your child and their tomorrow.
No happy memories yet to be made.
All you can do is retell your old stories.
As eyes look away and interest fades.

Your curse should be placed upon no one.
But just for a moment, you wish they could feel.
The depth of the pain that you carry.
But they can't imagine and they never will.

Left to reflect on your loss in silence.
As conversation around you goes on.
They never mention the child that you're
grieving.
So afraid they'll remind you they're gone.

Two Worlds is a poem that describes the thin delicate line that separates tragedy and happiness. I know that prior to experiencing Brandon's suicide, I never imagined that life could turn on you so quickly. One minute you're happy and have your family and the next it can all just disappear. My whole life made the transition from triumph to tragedy in the course of an evening. At 5:00PM, I had my son and dreams of the future, and by 7:00pm, I was left to cope with his suicide. That was the night I made my transition from one world into the other, and as suicide survivors we have all crossed that chasm separating Heaven from hell. We no longer have to wonder what it would be like if tragedy were to strike, because it already has, and we are living with the consequences every day. Sadly, we are all too aware that there are two worlds.

Two Worlds

Some people face tragedies.
While others never will.
Pain most could not imagine.
Others are forced to feel.

Two worlds that are thinly divided.
Merely a phone call apart.
A lifetime full of happiness.
Or living with a broken heart.

Heaven and hell.
Coexisting in the same spaces.
The blessed have their children to hold.
The cursed can only dream of their faces.

So appreciate every moment.
Every second you get to spend.
With those you love so dearly.
You never know when it will end.

Destroyer is a poem that draws on all of my experiences with suicide. In this poem I view suicide as a deadly predator that is always lurking and waiting for a moment of weakness. Suicide always reminds me of the famous Greek tale of the sirens song, luring innocent victims in with its captivating song for the sole purpose of destroying them. In our loved ones case, they had been seduced with the drama of suicide. They were so mesmerized by its deadly whispers that they didn't stop to consider the impact of their actions. If only our loved ones could have broken that deadly spell in time, then they would still be here and this book would not exist. Unfortunately, our loved ones never gained that moment of clarity, they never received that second chance at life. Now, we are the ones left behind to make sense of it all, an aspiration that we will never see fully realized in our lifetime.

Destroyer

Destroyer of the future.
Thy name is suicide.
You devour hopes and dreams.
As you conquer and divide.

Countless precious lives.
Are consumed by your flame.
You take away our loved ones.
And leave us here to blame.

You cloak yourself in darkness.
To shield you from the light.
Always watching and waiting.
Until the time is right.

Then in a moment of weakness.
You come in for the kill.
Erasing self- preservation.
In addition to free will.

And as another victim falls.
You escape into the night.
Taking all the answers with you.
As you vanish out of sight.

One of my favorite pictures of me and Brandon.

How Far is a poem that ponders various questions about Heaven. I never liked the thought that Brandon would still be able to see me. I don't believe that it could possibly feel like Heaven if he was forced to watch me mourn his passing. Instead, I like to picture Brandon surrounded by loving angels, comforted by the knowledge that we will soon be together again. Although I don't know what awaits us in Heaven. I do believe that all of our loved ones will be there to greet us. I know that after living here on earth as a suicide survivor, we deserve the peace of Heaven more than anyone. So please don't lose faith, I know in my heart that one day we will see our loved ones again.

How Far

How far must I go.
To get to where you are.
Are you always near me.
Or beyond some distant star.

Can you hear me as I'm crying.
In the darkest hours of night.
Or is it muted by the wings of angels.
As you're embraced by their light.

Do you know how much I miss you.
Or just that we'll meet again.
I hope that it's the latter.
I want you to be happy until then.

Please know that I'll always love you.
With every piece of my broken heart.
Until we meet one day in heaven.
To live forever and never part.

Orphaned is a poem that describes the plight of a bereaved parent. In the poem, I refer to us as homesick children. I believe that is the perfect description. As long as I'm busy and concentrating on something else then I can get by, but at nighttime when it's just me and my thoughts. That's when the longing for my son is the strongest. In the beginning this feeling was almost unbearable, but it has dulled quite a bit with time. I still miss my son terribly, but now I try to concentrate on that glad day when I will see him once again. Another focus of the poem is the search for meaning you will undergo after your child's suicide. You will somehow want to let the world know that your child existed, that they were so much more than just a tragic statistic. This book is my attempt at just that, it is my way of reaching out to comfort others in Brandon's memory. In time you will find your own way of honoring your child's memory, until then just try and focus on healing your broken heart.

Orphaned

We are lost among the living.
Orphaned parents that search in vain.
For purpose and for meaning.
To distract us from the pain.

Much like homesick children.
We try to occupy our minds.
To shield us from the reality.
That we've been left behind.

Our lives defy the normal order.
The future is eclipsed by the past.
Yearning for yesterday, not tomorrow.
Each day more empty than the last.

No hope of solace in this lifetime.
Our children have crossed over death's divide.
Walking wounded through this existence.
Until we see them on the other side.

Things is a poem that was written out of frustration. I see so many people going through life trying to accumulate more and more things, when it is the people in our lives that we should be focusing on. I think it takes a profound loss to wake you up to this fact. It takes something that powerful to make you see how much your family really means to you. I still have most of Brandon's belongings, but they don't offer me any consolation when I'm crying. I receive no comfort from holding them when I'm lonely. Those are the times when you need your loved ones. Material possessions have no capacity to show love or compassion. Objects will never be able to take the place of our loved ones, because after all they are just things.

Things

Keepsakes and belongings.
Are all that remain.
They offer no comfort.
They can't ease my pain.

Childhood mementos.
Now too hard to see.
Only serve to remind me.
How life used to be.

Objects are heartless.
And hold no relief.
They have no power.
To lessen my grief.

Things are just things.
They can't dry one tear.
So cherish your loved ones.
While they're still here.

Your Memory is a poem that really needs no explanation. It is simply me longing to have my son back by my side. Brandon was fifteen and still lived at home, so I will never stop expecting him to come walking down the stairs to tell me goodnight. It seems like it has been forever since the last time I hugged him and gave him the usual kiss on his forehead. He always complained and asked me why I kissed him there. That's when I would ask him if he preferred a kiss on the cheek. Needless to say, he said the forehead was fine. Little memories like that, are what makes life bearable.

Your Memory

You are Gone but not forgotten.
You will live on in my heart.
Death may have us separated.
But can't keep us apart.

You're in my every thought.
I miss your voice, I miss your smile.
Forced to go on living.
Thinking about you all the while.

Time may dry the tears.
But fails to dull the pain.
A survivor with a wounded spirit.
Whose affliction will remain.

Until my journey's over.
And I return to your side.
I live my life in your honor.
With your memory as my guide.

Nighttime is a poem that describes the struggle to get through the night when consumed with grief. After the suicide of a loved one, being alone with your thoughts can be a very scary place to be. I can still remember those first few months. That's when I viewed bedtime as more of a punishment than an escape. I would lie there for hours reliving the day that Brandon completed suicide. Praying that it was all just a bad dream, and this would go on until my mind and body would finally succumb to exhaustion. I would usually wake up a few short hours later to realize that this nightmare was real and Brandon was actually gone. I can still remember that sharp piercing pain that accompanied that realization. It has taken some time, but I no longer dread nighttime. My sleep has slowly returned to a somewhat normal pattern, and Brandon's suicide is something I no longer dwell on, but the fact that I lost him is still the first thing on my mind every time I wake up.

Nighttime

As darkness falls around me.
My mind dwells on days gone by.
I thought I had you for a lifetime.
But now I'm left to wonder why.

Tortured by old memories.
That haunt me every night.
Reliving the day I lost you.
If I could only make it right.

But my pleas for redemption.
Are made relentlessly in vain.
No remedy for my affliction.
A shattered heart so full of pain.

Sleep finally offers its reprieve.
Granting me rest until the dawn.
That's when the cruel light of daybreak.
Will reveal that you're still gone.

Holidays was written around Christmas time. That is a very difficult time for all suicide survivors. It seems like the entire world is filled with joy, everyone but you that is. If this is going to be your first holiday without your loved one, I would encourage you to come up with some plans for those days, even if you plan on ignoring the holidays. The simple act of planning to do so, will help to ease some of the anxiety you will feel on those days. You will usually find that the days leading up to the holiday, are typically more difficult than the holiday itself. I always try to tell myself that it's just another day. After all, I am without my son every day. That thought usually helps me to put everything in perspective.

Holidays

They'll be no merry Christmas.
No New Year's full of cheer.
They're just days on the calendar.
Now that you're not here.

A home once so full of love.
Has been all but destroyed.
It seems so empty and cold.
Without your smile to fill the void.

Thoughts of facing another year.
Overwhelm my broken heart.
I wish I could stop time.
Rewind it and restart.

But I know it's not to be.
I believe in miracles no more.
I will forever be a stranger.
To the life I lived before.

Scream is a poem inspired by my preferred method of anger management. There is nothing that relieves built up stress and anger better than letting out a nice loud primal scream. It might seem kind of strange the first time you do it, but nothing works better for releasing pent up tension. If you don't feel comfortable screaming for everyone to hear, you can always scream into a pillow to muffle the sound. Just trust me, and the next time you can feel that pressure start to build. Find yourself a nice private place, take a long deep breath and scream.

Scream

When I'm all alone.
My thoughts always turn to you.
Can't hold back my emotions.
I scream it can't be true.

I feel the pressure build.
There's desperation in the air.
I'd give anything to hold you.
I scream it's so unfair.

The flashbacks overwhelm me.
Trapped with nowhere to go.
Thinking of that awful day.
All I can scream is NO.

I pretend that everything's okay.
When other people are around.
But inside the storm still rages.
With screams that never make a sound.

Envy is a poem that describes an emotion that as a bereaved parent, I'm not really proud of. Sadly whenever I see a family that is happy and whole, I can't help but to feel very envious. It might not be something people talk about, but it is perfectly normal to feel this way after your world has been torn apart by suicide. So don't be too hard on yourself if you find that you're feeling the same way. You have suffered a life altering loss and it's only human to wish that you could somehow get your old life back. You're not truly jealous of the other families, you just miss your loved one and want them back. There is no need to feel guilty if you have had these moments of envy. You are simply grieving the loss of your family member, and this feeling is completely natural.

Envy

Deep within my being.
Lurks a jealousy that goes untold.
Hearing of other people's children.
While mine's not here to hold.

It's a weakness I don't share.
But one I can't control.
I try not to indulge it.
This envy of the whole.

I watch as happy families.
Pass by without a care.
While I'm left all alone.
With love I'll never share.

I'm not proud of these emotions.
But they exist and they are real.
So I will keep them to myself.
And go on hiding how I feel.

Torment is a poem about my struggles with God. I can't help but to cry out for answers sometimes. I try to be brutally honest in my poetry and this poem is a perfect example. Don't feel bad if you have experienced the same feelings. God is big enough to take our anger and questions. I'm sure that God prefers honest questioning over feigned praise. You can't keep secrets from God. Just remember, you're not telling him anything that he doesn't already know. So just be honest and tell God exactly how you feel. It might not change your situation, but it can help to temporarily ease your mind.

Torment

I keep crying out to God.
Please take away my pain.
But my pleas are met with silence.
As hope and faith quickly wane.

You watch it all from a distance.
Indifferent witness to my demise.
Refusing to offer any assistance.
No response is your reply.

I've got nothing left to lose.
So I speak freely without fear.
Prove to me you're out there.
Show me that you're near.

Living in fear of my own thoughts.
Tortured by visions I'll never tell.
My hands still grasping for heaven.
As I sink further into hell.

Truth is a poem that expresses my longing to return to my old life, back to the time when suicide was merely a word that I avoided talking about. Return to a time when my mind was at peace and I still had my son by my side, before suicide claimed all of my hopes and dreams. When it was still simply an embarrassing incident from my past, but all of this is merely a childish wish now. Once suicide divides your life into before and after, no amount of wishing can turn back the clock. This new normal has no connection and little resemblance to our old lives, and learning to accept that can take years. I will always yearn for the days when I held my son in my arms and all the world was right, but sadly that is now something that is only possible in my dreams.

Truth

I stumbled into this nightmare.
On just an ordinary day.
Now it seems I'm trapped forever.
The pain refusing to go away.

My Tomorrows have been stolen.
So I live in days gone by.
There I can just be with you.
No need to ask the question why.

But reality always intrudes.
Reciting truths I choose to deny.
My son could never leave me.
My boy could never die.

I refuse to accept the facts.
And the future that will never be.
So I retreat into the past.
Where I can have you here with me.

This Place is a glimpse into the painful world of child loss. I touch on the sleepless nights and the overwhelming guilt you will feel. You will beat yourself up for every perceived mistake that was made while raising your child, and as parents we are our own harshest critics. Please don't let my poetry discourage you though. I gather my inspiration from every moment spent since losing Brandon, so a lot of my poems reflect emotions that I experienced years ago, but no matter how many years pass. I would gladly trade in this new normal in an instant, if I could return to my old life. That is something that will never change, no matter how much time passes.

This Place

I sit gazing out the window.
Blankly staring into space.
Not noticing the world outside.
As I reflect upon this place.

The sleepless nights are endless.
Their almost more than I can take.
Pondering all the mistakes I've made.
As I'm lying wide awake.

No matter how much support.
I still feel so all alone.
I don't want to deal with this.
I just want to go back home.

But I'm trapped in this new normal.
Like some strange and foreign land.
Only another parent of an angel.
Could ever begin to understand.

My Wish is a poem that offered me a few hours of escape while I was writing it. I'm sure everyone that has suffered a loss to suicide wishes they could turn back the clock and have a second chance at life. Can you imagine how much more appreciative we would be of those we lost. Every second spent with them would be a treasure. Sadly this is not possible, but one day we will get our wish and our loved ones will again be by our side. Then all of the worries and questions we have will finally be forgotten, but until then I will keep on wishing.

My Wish

If I could be granted three wishes.
They would all be just the same.
You would be here to answer.
Whenever I call out your name.

I can't imagine the feeling.
Of having you back once again.
To dream at last of the future.
So tired of remembering when.

My hurt would disappear in an instant.
With one look at your beautiful face.
All of the years spent without you.
Your smile would completely erase.

My mind would no longer be troubled.
My soul would know comfort and peace.
Once you were back in my arms.
All of my questions would finally cease.

Empty Chair was written in response to Brandon's high school refusing to have an empty chair for him at graduation. At first I was angry, until I realized that everyone he knew will always remember him, they will never need an empty chair to remind them of the person they lost. They will always be aware of his absence. I believe that gestures such as these can be very comforting, but are unnecessary to those that loved him. In my opinion, simply speaking of him is the most honoring thing that we could do. That way he continues to live on through the memories we share. That is why I will always speak Brandon's name and share my stories of him. That way, people can come to know the boy, that I will forever be proud to call my son.

Empty Chair

An empty chair to remember.
Someone no one could forget.
A cause for celebration.
Now overshadowed by regret.

Your smile should be present.
Not confined to the past.
Memories console for the moment.
But the comfort never lasts.

The sound of your voice.
Is one I long to hear.
The silence can be deafening.
And the truth is all too clear.

For the rest of my days.
You will be absent from my side.
No empty chair is needed.
To remind me that you died.

Searching was written during a very difficult time. It expresses my disbelief over losing Brandon. In the beginning I would tell myself that he was visiting a friend or had just temporarily gone away somewhere. I would think of almost anything to avoid admitting the truth. Grief has a way of blinding us to reality. It tries to convince us that it was all just a bad dream and we will wake up eventually. I have now finally come to accept that my son is not returning to me, but I know that one day I will go to where he is, and all of my searching will finally be over.

Searching

In spite of reality.
I'm searching for you.
You cannot be gone.
It cannot be true.

We had so much to do.
So much left to say.
But it all just ended.
On that terrible day.

One permanent action.
In a moment of haste.
Watched my future implode.
My dreams laid to waste.

Now left with nothing.
I pretend it's not real.
And continue my quest.
To resurrect and reveal.

Trapped in this madness.
Grief has me so blind.
Looking for something.
That's not there to find.

Mirage is a poem that asks a question I have heard countless survivors ask. Was my old life simply a mirage? Of course our old lives were not mirages, but at times it sure feels like it. Suicide creates this illusion because there is such a stark difference between before and after. It is almost like a dividing line between Heaven and hell. Our old lives were not perfect, but they can seem that way when contrasted with life after suicide. This feeling of disbelief is almost universal after suffering a loss to suicide. Just be patient, in time this feeling will fade just like all other facets of grief.

Mirage

Was it real or imagined?
The life I knew before.
Regardless of the answer.
I long to return once more.

So tired of feeling restless.
Growing weary from the wait.
Hoping you'll come back to me.
Unable to accept my fate.

Left to live out my tragedy.
Without a chance to make things right.
My happiness forever stolen.
Since you vanished from my sight.

All alone on the inside.
Even though others share in my pain.
Robbed of the life I'd planned on.
Only shattered hopes and dreams remain.

Fear is a poem that expresses a worry that I once had. I lost Brandon at the age of fifteen and I used to constantly worry that his memories would not be enough to last me my entire life. I also feared that a lot of my memories of him were lost due to the shock of suicide. It has taken a few years, but all of my happy memories of Brandon have come flooding back. Now, I know that his memory will be with me no matter how long I live. He will live on forever in my heart and mind, and no amount of time will ever be able to change that. Memories are timeless and unending, as long as I'm alive his memory will be also.

Fear

The days all feel so heartless.
The nights last far too long.
Without you here beside me.
Everything just seems so wrong.

All of the hopes and goals.
That used to urge me on.
Now all seem so pointless.
Without you they're all gone.

Being pushed into the future.
While holding onto the past.
Stretching your memory thinner.
So worried that it won't last.

Fearing we will become strangers.
Due to the years we've spent apart.
My mind knows that it won't happen.
But try telling that to my broken heart.

Deception is a poem that is very similar to Mask as far as inspiration is concerned. It is about our desire to put on a happy front for the world, regardless of how much pain we are experiencing. I believe that one reason this occurs is because this. Most people think that after a few short months, we should just get over our loved one's death and move on. Since we are still in a great deal of pain, we naturally pretend to be okay. In doing so you are only prolonging your grief, so cry if you need to cry. If you make those around you uncomfortable, then that is their problem. Grief is a perfectly normal reaction to losing someone we love, and crying is simply an expression of that love. Please don't get discouraged and just remember this helpful piece of advice. Grief cannot be rushed. It must be felt, so don't hold back the tears for anyone.

Deception

I walk among the living.
But it's all just make believe.
I do it to survive.
I don't do it to deceive.

I will say that I'm okay.
As inside I fall apart.
Don't be surprised if I seem distant.
I'm existing with half a heart.

It all seems so unfair.
How people expect me to move on.
Just go on like nothing happened.
Even though my child is gone.

But there's no use in explaining.
They can't understand my pain.
So I will continue my deception.
Until death offers its refrain.

Without Hope is a poem that was written during a very difficult time in my life. I was trying to ween myself off of my depression medication which I had been taking since losing Brandon. I had reached a point to where I thought I could function without it. Well I was wrong, it was like I had been transported to the past and had just lost Brandon all over again. Since that time I have realized that there is no shame in taking medication to cope with the loss of my son, so if you are currently under a doctor's care. I urge you to consult with them before making any changes to your medication. Which is something that I neglected to do, but from that depression came this poem. Which sounds a lot like some of my earlier ones. It truly conveys the hopelessness you feel after losing someone to suicide, but even in the midst of that depression. I still held onto the hope of Heaven. When all of this hurt and pain will finally be taken away, so if you're having an especially hard time just remember that you are never truly without hope.

Without Hope

What remains of this life?
When all hope is stripped away.
Laboring through the endless hours.
That comprise each empty day.

Looking for an explanation.
How did I end up left behind?
With no dreams or aspirations.
To distract my beleaguered mind.

Now I'm simply a silent witness.
Watching my life as it passes me by.
Just waiting for it to be over.
Tired of hearing myself asking why.

I search in vain for a purpose.
Or some reason to live on without you.
I know this was not your intention.
But that doesn't make it any less true.

Only death can open the doorway.
Which will lead me at last to your side.
And my body can finally be buried.
So long after my spirit has died.

Numb is a poem that expresses emotions that every suicide survivor knows all too well. That feeling of having your life stolen and being left behind to suffer. It also mentions the loss of control we feel after we lose someone we love to suicide. Before losing Brandon, I just took it for granted that he would always be there. I made plans for the future without any worries of them being disrupted by tragedy. In short, I felt as if I was in control of my own destiny, and then suicide entered the picture and shattered those illusions. Now, I take nothing for granted. Because I know just how quickly it can all be taken away. It is a realization that I wish everyone could come to, but sadly it usually takes something as devastating as suicide loss in order to get our attention.

Numb

Suicide has stolen.
A piece of my soul.
And all of the illusions.
I once held of control.

Claiming the life.
Which I once knew.
Ripped it apart.
As it tore it in two.

Leaving me restless.
And yearning for peace.
No end to this torment.
The questions won't cease.

All I am now.
Is a cold empty shell.
Searching for heaven.
As I'm wandering through hell.

I Miss You is a poem that simply laments on my longing for my son. There are times when I miss him so badly that I think I can't go on. Brandon was so much more than just my son. He was my best friend and workout partner. He was my reason for striving to be a better provider and most importantly, he was my future. That is what we all grieve more than any other aspect of suicide loss. We had imagined what our lives would be like and now all those dreams are shattered by suicide. It is this loss of expectations that we must now deal with on a daily basis. Not to mention their birthday and anniversary date which you will have to deal with every year. Then there is the emptiness of the holidays without your loved one. Time can help to lessen the impact on those days, but will never be able to take away this longing we have to see our loved ones again. No matter how many years pass, we will always miss them deeply.

I Miss You

You were my whole world.
My pride and joy.
Such a beautiful soul.
You were my boy.

Now you're in Heaven.
Right by God's side.
I'm left here broken.
With all this time.

How can I accept?
That I must carry on.
That's just so hard.
Now that you're gone.

In a world so cruel.
This one thing is true.
No one could imagine.
How much I miss you.

Time is a poem that is about just that. It expresses how suicide alters our perception of time. It may seem like we haven't seen our loved ones in forever, yet the suicide seems like it happened yesterday. I lost Brandon in October of 2010, and I can still remember that time period as clearly as I can last week. To my mind, it would seem just as natural to wake up in the morning and it still be 2010. The memory loss which accompanies a death by suicide, only serves to exacerbate this problem. Now looking back, the first few years after losing Brandon seem almost like the lost years. I still went about my day to day activities, but my mind was on auto pilot. Now several years later, time is starting to synchronize with my mind once again. Although I believe a part of me will forever be stranded in 2010, searching for my son.

Time

As another year passes.
That hasn't known you.
I rebel against reality.
Too bad to be true.

Seems like forever.
Yet still like days.
Time keeps on ticking.
My heartache still stays.

Your name's rarely spoken.
Unless it's by me.
Amazing how cruel.
Well-meaning people can be.

I'm stuck in the past.
And still can't move on.
I will never accept.
The fact that you're gone.

My Mind is a poem that expresses how the thought of Brandon completing suicide never once entered my mind. I could have listed a million things concerning Brandon that I worried about, and suicide would not have been on that long list. Why would I be alarmed about suicide? I had a happy and well-adjusted son that would never consider such a thing. I always viewed suicide as something that only affected certain types of people. Little did I know that suicide doesn't discriminate in its quest to destroy. It will cross racial, socio-economic, and nearly any other boundaries you try to place on it. It is a killer that can strike any one of us without exception, given the right set of circumstances.

My Mind

Once upon a time.
In days and years gone by.
The fear that I would lose you.
Would rarely, if ever cross my mind.

When I thought of what could happen.
What could steal you from my arms?
In all the different scenarios.
Suicide never even once, entered my mind.

In the wake of your departure.
When my world came crashing down.
That tragic day just kept replaying.
Over and over, in my mind.

When the disbelief and shock.
Were slowly fading from my view.
I feared all of the good times.
Would somehow be erased, from my mind.

Now that time has dulled my grief,
And the tears no longer flow.
Your memory is all that keeps me going.
And now has a home forever, in my mind.

Fate is a poem that ponders the question, were our loved ones destined to die by suicide? Did we lose them for some mystical purpose, or to teach us a valuable lesson? Personally, I don't accept either of the above statements. I simply believe that freewill and circumstance combined to form a perfect storm, which culminated in our loved one's suicide. I choose to believe that it was simply an irreversible mistake, which was made in a moment of weakness. Otherwise I would be forced to accept that my son's entire life, was nothing more than a tragic story with a forgone conclusion. And try as I may, I just cannot bring myself to believe that a loving God would allow such a thing to happen. However just like all other questions surrounding suicide loss, this too will remain unanswered during this lifetime.

Fate

Everything happens for a reason.
People just love to say.
But there could never be a reason.
For you leaving me this way.

Life is not planned out.
There's no such thing as fate.
It's simply chance and timing.
As both converge on a deadly date.

And God did not permit this.
No one is predestined to die.
My son made a terrible mistake.
Leaving me behind to wonder why.

Your words have implications.
Everyone's life is not as planned.
Only someone that's lost it all.
Could ever begin to understand.

We Walk was written specifically for suicide prevention and awareness walks. I encourage you to share it at your local walk or event. In writing it, I wanted to sum up all of the reasons I participate in events such as these. You will never fully realize how prevalent suicide is until you witness a literal sea of survivors that have all joined together for a common goal. Which is to help erase the stigma surrounding suicide. It is a very reassuring feeling to be amongst a crowd of people that are all facing the same challenge of suicide loss. We have made great strides in the fight against the stigma and shame of suicide, and public events like these are one of the major reasons why. If you have a walk in your area, I would highly recommend that you consider attending. You will find it to be both comforting and empowering.

We Walk

We walk to remember.
To honor those we've lost.
To keep alive their memories.
Regardless of the cost.

We walk to overcome.
To prove we will survive.
We could have chosen surrender.
But yet we're still alive.

We walk to break the stigma.
To rebel against the shame.
There are no faceless victims.
Our loved ones had a name.

We walk to prevent.
To spare others from this pain.
As long as suicide exists.
Our perseverance will remain.

Final Thoughts

You have been through hell, but you're still standing. You have lost a piece of your heart, yet you live on. Be proud of yourself, you have had every reason to quit, but you have instead chosen to survive. You have experienced the horror of suicide loss and now know a depth of pain that most could not imagine. So stay strong, and I promise you it will get more bearable with time. The pain will lessen, and all those happy memories that you thought were lost will come flooding back. You will build a new normal, and although you will never be the same person you once were, that doesn't mean that you will never feel happiness again. Your smile will return, and so will the laughter that you thought was lost forever. But in your eyes, there will always be that hint of sadness. You have lost someone very dear to you and time will never make that reality go away. Your loss to suicide has now become a part of who you are, and while it doesn't define you. It has helped to shape you into the person which you have become. You are a much more caring person, because of the suffering which you have endured. Now you will feel a special kinship with the broken, a strong desire to help ease the pain of others. It is this newfound sense of compassion that will allow you to move forward and make a difference in this world. Then, when you finally get to Heaven and see your loved one once again. You will bring with you a long line of people that you have helped along the way. Because of your undying love, you were able to leave a legacy of kindness and compassion. It is these things that will define your loved ones memory, not their suicide. I hope that this book has both inspired and consoled you. So please, take this tragedy and turn it into something positive.

Made in the USA
Middletown, DE
01 December 2019

79753487R00071